Thoughts from the Stand

A Unique Collection of Poetry
About Hunting and the Outdoors
by Brent Bacon

Thoughts from the Stand
A Unique Collection of Poetry
About Hunting and the Outdoors

Written by Brent Bacon
All photographs and altered photographs
are by the author.

Published by
Lone Wolf Publishers
Lewisburg, Pennsylvania 17837
www.lonewolfpublishers.com

Contact Brent Bacon at:
lonewolf@lonewolfpublishers.com

Artwork by
LeAnna Clark
Contact information at: lonewolfpublishers.com

ISBN 13: 978-0-9793908-0-7

Manufactured in the United States of America

First Printing May 2007

My story's as old as the mountains,
And yet maybe older still.
It's about the pursuit and the chase,
the everlovin' thrill and the kill.

THE HUNTING POET

Quite often people ask me if I write while hunting and in the woods. The answer is not if I don't have to. Here is another answer in rhyme.

Rhymin' & Huntin'

Now I'm here to tell ya
this rhymin' thing's alright.
I think about it all the time,
ever' minute day and night.

But huntin's my reason fer livin',
an' I wouldn't give it up fer nuttin'.
But I will give up this rhymin'
if it interferes with my huntin'.

DEDICATION

DAD
That's me.
The little one.
My hunting days
had just begun.
Dad & me . . .
we were one.
Inseparable,
Boy, we had fun.
Dad is gone.
His hunting days are done.
Some days I take a walk and
go hunting with his gun.

The memories come back,
they always bring a tear.
Of Dad & me a hunting . . .
out there hunting deer.
The memories of Dad
that's what keeps him near.
Those memories of Dad . . .
that I hold so dear.

Dedicated
to the memory of my Father

ACKNOWLEDGEMENTS

Thanks are in order for many people. There are so many that have played a part in my life and the creation of this book.

Thank you Rod Nichols for all your help and support at Poems Place, our old gathering place in cyberspace. I am honored that you wrote the preface.

Just a word about Rod: Here in the East where the majority of people will be reading my book, Cowboy Poetry is not known by many. However, out west, in the world of Cowboy Poetry, Rod is an icon.

Rod is a native Texan and cowboy poet performing at cowboy gatherings, rodeos, fairs, and schools. He was the first "Lariat Laureate" of CowboyPoetry.com. He has contributed to many magazines and books, some of which are: *The Lazy B* by Hon. Sandra Day O'Connor, *American Food Festivals* by Becky Mecuri, *The Big Roundup* by Cowboypoetry.com, *A Little Bit Of Texas* his own book, and his newest release *Drover Diaries*. Magazines and newspapers include: *The Wyoming Companion*, University of Wyoming, *Rope Burns*, Academy Of Western Artists, *The American Quarter Horse Journal*, *American Cowboy* and a *Cowboy History And Performing Society CD* (C.H.A.P.S.) an anthology of cowboy poetry. His other CD's include, *In God's Hands, Cowboy Christmas Mem'ries, Yep, A Little Bit More Of Texas*, and *The Big Roundup* at Cowboypoetry.com

Rod is the recipient of many prestigious awards, some of which include: 1st Lariat Laureate of Cowboypoetry.com, a Robert W. Service Award, an H.G. Wells writing award and he was a contributing author to the *Big Roundup* which won the Best Cowboy Poetry Book for the year 2001. His book *A Little Bit Of Texas* received a Will Rogers Medallion for 2003 from the Academy Of Western Artists.

Rod Nichols has a website and his work is available through it: http://www.geocities.com/rodnichols.geo/cowboy.html.

Special thanks go to Ken Piper for writing the Foreword. When Ken expressed an appreciation for my work, I thought who better to write the Foreword for the book than a fellow Pennsylvanian, even though he now resides in Alabama.

Ken Piper grew up in Pennsylvania, hunting public-land whitetails with his father, Ken Sr. He graduated from Penn State in 1987 with a bachelor's in Journalism and worked in newspapers for eight years before becoming a magazine editor.

In 2000, Buckmasters called to see if Ken would be interested in editing its website. So he loaded up the truck and moved to Alabama.

Ken is now the managing editor of Buckmasters Whitetail Magazine. He is an avid bowhunter, and whitetails are still his hunting passion.

Thanks to my wife, Su, who tolerates me, my pursuits, and my mess, and still keeps me around.

A special thanks goes out to the artist, LeAnna Clark. Once she became involved, she was a major positive motivational force in my efforts to get this in print.

I thank the fine folks at The Pennsylvania Reader, for publishing my poems.

Also, I thank the "United Bowhunters of Pennsylvania" for publishing my poetry in their monthly publication Pennsylvania Bowhunting.

Especially, I want to thank all of the hunting buddies past, present, and future. There is very special bond which develops between hunters during this age old pursuit. Thanks for the inspiration and the memories.

Thanks go to all of my family (related or not) and friends that provided much needed support and encouragement and to those that shared my excitement and enthusiasm, and graciously tolerated my impromptu poetry readings.

Thanks to my father, Maynard, who passed away in May of 2000, for instilling in me the values, respect and wisdom of man's relationship with the land and it's inhabitants, for the hunting memories, and the many long conversations while doing the milking and other chores on the farm. His presence is dearly missed and warmly remembered.

And most of all, I thank GOD, for without HIM none of this would be possible.

I apologize if I have overlooked anyone; it was certainly not intentional.

INTRODUCTION

Growing up in North Central Pennsylvania on a dairy farm, my ties with the land were instilled at an early age. This collection of poems is my way of expressing what is ingrained in me, not just a sport, but a way of life. Some of these things are universal and some are from my perspective, given my surroundings and influences growing up in Potter County, Pennsylvania.

I started writing poetry in February of 2001. My first poem was *"The Bowhunter"*. Writing poetry became quite a passion for a few years and now I seem to have slowed down. I still write poetry occasionally; however, my muse visits less often nowadays. The thoughts to which I am most passionate and would really like to write about are the most difficult to express. I hope as you read these poems, first and foremost, you enjoy them.

Secondly, I would like you to sense the love and passion for the outdoors and the desire to pass it on. If people don't use and enjoy our resources responsibly, they will have no desire to protect them and no respect for the world as it should be. Too many people want to change the world to fit their needs. They don't seem to realize that the world is as big as it is, and they think they can control everything. The earth will be here long after we are gone. Instead of working with nature, man has become a cancer to the earth. I think that's obvious; however, mankind needs to be reminded.

I guess that if my poetry is to have a goal or a purpose, aside from entertaining you, (And yes, "The Arts" have purpose aside from entertaining), it would be to speak the unspoken, to take all of the things that we find so difficult to put into words about why we hunt, and somehow illustrate it or put it on paper, to define the indefinable; and at times by just describing the little things that surround the hunting experience, sometimes not so directly, but through metaphors and analogies, the way man has communicated complex thoughts down through countless ages.

All of these little accessories, if you will, contribute to the hunting experience, the little things that we all take for granted: the sunrise or sunset, birds chirping, and the smells of nature. The list goes on, not the least of which are the bonds between hunters and the memories that we relive as we are hunting.

Then there are all of the things that we may think about if we were forced to think: the excitement, the adrenalin rush, and the comradery. The comradery is probably the first element to be recognized, and yet it is still not fully understood. Just what is it about this activity that creates a bond that is sometimes closer than blood?

It is not my attempt to explain these concepts in any way, only to illustrate and create fond remembrances of this beloved, lifelong, and sacred activity that is nowadays coming under scrutiny by people who have no idea what the hunting experience entails or means to those of us that participate in it.

We are being forced into rationalizing our "sport," or as I prefer to call it, "our lifestyle." But that is not a bad thing. To answer the question, "Why do we hunt" causes us to question some of our deepest held beliefs. Since it is obvious that the sole reason we hunt is not for food alone; meat can be purchased at grocery stores. Is it to fill some primordial urge? Or is there some value in understanding the life that is given to sustain ours?

So, don't begrudge the anti-hunting community for asking and wanting us to explain. Thank them for the chance to consider these things, for you will be a better person and more thoughtful hunter having done so.

After it is all said and done, I may not have answered any questions, defined the indefinable, or found the words that have escaped us for so long. I will have, however, spent many countless hours on this, and hopefully caused you to think about it. And that! **is always**, a good thing.

Good Luck and Good Hunting!

PREFACE

In wilderness lies the preservation of man, and in man lies the means to preserve wilderness. This was the unmistakable feeling I had as I read the final page of Brent Bacon's collection of poems and photos, *Thoughts From The Stand.* The relationship between the hunter and the wilderness is both unique and universal. While the individual experiences a private moment and feeling, he is not alone in the global sense of every man who goes forth as the hunter.

Fortunate, indeed, is the reader who ventures forth with Brent Bacon into the great outdoors and shares some very special moments. The author has an artist's eye and a poet's heart as his photography and verse testify. You do not need to be a hunter to appreciate the up-close feeling of being there. Even the most ardent foe of hunting will find much to appreciate in the bond between man and the wilderness. As the author says, "We must strive to preserve and not destroy the beauty and wonder of nature."

There in the fading light
I spot a buck off to my right
I struggle with my sight
but it just isn't right.
I have no regret
that I passed on the shot tonight
just respect and the fact
that I was privileged with the sight.

I feel privileged to have read Brent Bacon's work and to share with you, the reader, some wonderful moments ahead. Good reading my friends and may you come to know the wonder of the wilderness.

Rod Nichols
Cowboy Poet

FOREWORD

For most of us, it's not possible to put our thoughts and feelings about hunting into words. The emotions are either too strong or too personal to share.

Whether it's from Pennsylvania roots or just a love of hunting and the outdoors, Brent Bacon's *"Thoughts From The Stand"* captured those emotions for me.

Brent includes everything from the quiet moments on stand in the dark, to the thrill of sending an arrow on its way, to the heartbreak of watching your favorite hunting spot turned into a housing development -- and even a few things I had felt but forgotten.

While the essence of hunting will always remain a personal and close-kept treasure in my heart, it's good to know there are writers out there like Brent who can remind us that we're not alone.

Ken Piper
Managing Editor
Buckmaster's
Whitetail Magazine

Table of Contents

MORNIN'

A hunter sits in the cold and the dark,
silent and listening. His back to the bark.
He's climbed this tree many times before.
Following the trail of a big buck's lore.

Fleeting glimpses, rarely seen,
More mystical than anything.
Birds are chirping. It's still dark.
In the distance a dog will bark.

The horizon glows in the eastern sky.
Trees take shape. An owl glides by.
The drone of a truck on a far away hill.
This makes the hunt; it's not the kill!

THE BOWHUNTER

Perched on a hilltop, far and away
from the hustle and bustle of life's everyday.
Up in a tree, or down on the ground,
he's in before daylight, without a sound.

In blackness he's waiting for daylight's reprieve.
Gray takes over as darkness leaves.
He has forgotten life's problems; his troubles are gone.
He is one with nature, at the break of dawn.

The shades of gray fuse with colors so bright.
The woods in the fall are a breathtaking sight.
Relaxed yet ready, his bow in his hand,
awestruck by nature, just one grain of sand.

A shake of the head, a silent sigh,
the stillness is broken, leaves rustle nearby.
His heart is beating, first lightly then stronger.
His mind is racing, can't stand it much longer.

The sound is behind him. It's coming nearer.
Is it a squirrel? Or is it a deer?
Head turning slowly in the rhythm of the wood,
a squirrel is searching for his winter goods.

The squirrel scurries to bury a nut.
Acorns have fallen. The bucks are in rut.
His senses are primed. His heart won't slow,
A feeling only a hunter can know.

Primordial senses in overdrive;
it feels good just to be alive.
The leaves rustle again. This time it's for real.
A doe bounds out; ahh . . . it's no big deal.

She nudges leaves under his stand.
He regrips his bow with his left hand.
His predator instincts sense something's in store.
The hair stands on his neck, and he's ready once more.

The doe feeds on acorns this place doesn't lack.
Then she snaps her head up and looks over her back.
On the does back trail and off to his right,
Saplings start shaking. Oh, what a sight!

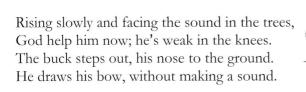

Rising slowly and facing the sound in the trees,
God help him now; he's weak in the knees.
The buck steps out, his nose to the ground.
He draws his bow, without making a sound.

At nineteen yards and quartering away,
the perfect shot any given day.
The arrow flew straight, and stuck in the ground.
Blood tip to tip and no buck around.

All hell broke loose on that autumn day.
With a hole in his chest, the buck runs away.
He sits down and leans back . . .
He tries to regain what he lacks.

No matter how many times he's been down this road,
It's always the same . . . Emotional overload.
He follows the trail through brush and pine,
Crouching low he spots a tine.

The feelings that go through a hunter's mind.
The emotions that flood, the ties that bind.

5

REMEMBERING

A frosty fall mornin', the bucks are in rut.
Better days are here; I feel it in my gut.
I leave the house, and walk up past the barn,
up across the fields, to the back of the farm.

My mind is at ease, as I stroll along,
remembering hunts, forever gone.
It's just before daybreak, and I head for my stand
sneakin' through the woods, with my bow in my hand.

I reach the tree, attach the stand,
climb twenty feet, survey the land.
I strap myself in, pull up my gear.
I settle in, and wait for deer.

The woods settle. I blend in.
Slowly, I drop powder* to check the wind.
It's all perfect, perfect as can be.
Me – sittin' here in this red oak tree.

My mind wanders. I reminisce.
I regret the hunts that I have missed.
For whatever reasons, I couldn't be there,
with family and friends, in the cool autumn air.

BB

Time spent hunting with family and friends
are times that you wish would never end.
Subtle movement, patches of brown.
Caught again . . . sittin' down.

A buck and a doe feeding along.
They haven't sensed that something is wrong.
Smugly, I sit and smile,
watching deer, all the while.

I think I have won today.
I've sat in this tree, and fooled my prey.
Some family and friends are gone now.
None of us last forever, that's clear.

Take my advice
and keep it near.
Make the most of your time;
get out and hunt deer.

*Powder: *Baking soda is often used to determine wind direction.*

THE ENCOUNTER

Sitting quietly, daydreaming, maybe?
In a stand with many memories,
the movie in your mind starts rolling.
A few years back a young buck came down that trail.
You passed on him, . . . and now, . . . now,
you feel his presence.

Goose bumps all over; hair stands on your neck.
Ghosting images, obscured by brush and stick.
He's older, wiser now; more myth than anything.
The feeling is gone. . . . Your heart won't slow.
Not quite sure of what you know.
Light fades. It's dark now.
You climb down and go home.

PRIVILEDGED

And here, in the fading light,
I spot the buck off to my right.
I struggle with my sight,
but it's just not right.

I have no regrets
that I passed on a shot tonight.
Just respect, and the fact,
that I was privileged with the sight.

Spring Turkey

And the early morning sky begins to glow.
There's a booming gobble in the valley below.
My heart starts pounding, adrenaline flow.
I ready myself for nature's show.

I notice the woods, mostly gray and brown,
as I find a tree and settle down.
Sprigs of green are all around,
and soon lush plants will abound.

Lest I forget why I am here,
the silence is broken by a gobble near.
He's coming fast, too fast I fear.
My call was too good, too crisp, too clear.

I put on my gloves and pull down my head net.
I look around but I don't see him yet.
I think to myself, "This is as good as it can get.
On this turkey's life, I am willing to bet."

He came in on a run; I thought he'd gobbled his last.
I sat in awe as he ran right past.
In retrospect, it all happened too fast.
Again that turkey kicked my butt!

11

Nature's AM Performance

Daylight breaking.
The drumming of a grouse.
May apples.
A woodpecker's shrill call.
New life all around.
A gobble down the hollow
completes the symphony
of sight and sound.

The End of the Day

Daylight subsides;
Long shadows hide.
A new night is born;
Tomorrow it will storm.

The movement is high;
there are deer nearby.
As I sit in my stand,
nature strikes up the band.

Night sounds abound,
as I smile at the sound.
If I stay here all night,
I'll be here at first light.

WHY

In the darkness, you sit waiting
high above the forest floor.
A new day's sun will soon be rising,
and you'll be hunting once more.

You sit. You wait.
You wonder. You listen.
How the dew on the leaves
At sunrise glistens.

Deer or no,
you're happy to be
sittin' there
in that tree.

You're full of emotion.
Your senses are piqued.
Sometimes you can't stand it,
and barely can speak.

Your thoughts year around
are of the woods in the fall.
To sit in a tree,
hear a lonesome crow call.

THE ULTIMATE PREDATOR

I sit, antlers in my hands,
staring at a lifeless body.
One that was . . . just moments ago, full of life.
A relationship as intimate as life and death,
for which I am responsible.
I had to do it.

Mixed emotions, victory, bittersweet success.
One dies that another may live.
This will not be the last time.
The cycle goes on.
If you need an explanation . . .
I am man.
I am . . .

Before the Hunt

Out in the dark, and lonesome,
in the woods and on the hills.
To be here anytime,
is how I get my thrills.

To feel a misty mornin'
damp upon my face.
To know that daylight's comin',
that night will leave no trace.

To stumble through the darkness
in the woods I know so well.
Memories, reality,
sometimes I just can't tell.

Sometimes I feel my father near,
though he's since passed away.
'twas springtime when he left us
on a sunny day in May.

The memories are many.
They're everywhere I look.
Sometimes, I think that I should
sit down and write a book.

In the spring we'd tap those maples.
In the summer we'd cut hay.
Early fall, the crops would call;
oats and corn would fill our day.

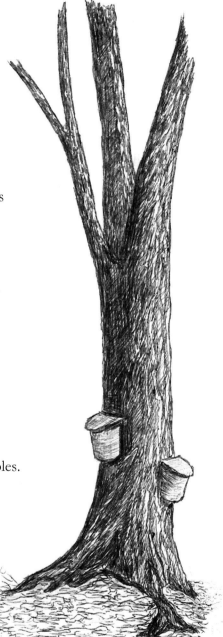

Yeah, the memories are many,
and the hunting ones are best.
Someday, I'll tell them all to you;
right now this needs a rest.

It's time to watch Ma Nature
do a painting in the sky.
She'll do it quick, so watch her
do it right before your eyes.

17

She starts with that black canvas
in the east o'er on that hill.
Subtle strokes of pink and orange;
she just can't get her fill.

She's paintin' fast and furious now;
you know she's doin' her best.
Using yellows now, and soon some blues,
chasin' darkness to the west.

Sunrise is just a bonus,
the day . . . is why I'm here.
I've got my Dad's ol' rifle;
now let's go hunt some deer.

After the Hunt

I sit here in the moonlight.
The huntin' day is done.
Can't say why I'm still here;
I guess it's just for fun.

The owl begins his hootin'.
A coyote courts the moon.
I'm enjoying this so much,
I may not leave too soon.

Ya know a couple hours ago,
'fore the sun went down,
The woods was full of life,
and the deer were all around.

I sit here in my treestand
just takin' it all in.
To leave right now and pass this up
would surely be a sin.

The turkeys, they have roosted,
they finally settled down.
And way off in the distance,
I hear the trucks leave town.

The far off sounds remind me
that I'm not really all alone.
It's gettin' late ya know;
I probably should get home.

I think of "real world progress(?)"
as supper calls my name.
And all the habitat there is,
to which development lays claim.

I guess I oughta go now.
I'm startin' to feel a chill.
Ya know there's somethin' 'bout these woods;
I just can't get my fill!

The Essence of Hunting

Fragrance adds dimensions
rarely thought of by our kind.
The very things we treasure most
are ones to which we're blind.

Have you ever smelled a buck in rut
when you were huntin' deer?
Or sniffed a lilac on the wind
as turkeys gobbled near?
How 'bout the smell of fresh tilled soil
as farmers plow their fields?
Then there's the smell of dryin' hay
as woodchucks are revealed.
The musty smell of fragrant woods
when huntin' in the fall.
This keeps me coming back each year
to answer nature's call.

The Moment!

And the pin settles
behind the shoulder's crease,
your mind is clear and focused
as the arrow is released.

Just My Luck

Perched here in this treestand,
staring into space.
Ponderin' the problems caused
by the human race.
It's the middle of the morning;
my mind is in first gear.
All I see are squirrels;
I suppose it's late for deer.

Jarred back to reality
from hunts of yesteryear.
Over there behind that tree,
movement, it's a deer.
Now, In all my years of huntin',
spent out here in the woods,
I've never seen a buck this big,
and never thought I would.

I like the simple pleasures;
they're somethin' to behold.
The sights, the sounds, the smells,
and touch, as memories unfold.
Now, this ol' buck beats anything
I think I ever saw.
He's really got me going.
My nerves are shot and raw.

My heart is beatin' louder
with every step he takes,
An now my darned ol' knees
have got the dreaded shakes.
He saunters in like the king of these parts;
he's the biggest I've ever seen.
He checks all trails and follows his nose
in search of a suitable queen.

Carefully lookin', everything in place,
as he steps with stealth and ease.
Old and wise and good with his eyes,
he sneaks through the hemlock trees.
His neck is thick, peak of the rut,
and he's tired from running all night.
Hair ruffled, prob'bly been in a fight,
an' I bet I could smell him if the wind was right.

The buck . . . stands there broadside,
and fifteen yards away.
Tears streamin' down my face,
as I curse my *worstest* day.
My heart sinks as I watch him go.
Today, I'm huntin' only doe.
Yesterday, it's just my luck,
I shot a scrawny six point buck.

PROGRESS?

I feel a bond with the mountain.
I sense her joy and pain.
I live beneath her canopy
and feel no need for gain.

Right now upon this very spot,
I stand with tear filled eyes.
I'll never hunt from here again,
for "Progress" broke my ties.

The "Progress" that a man inflicts . . .
I feel her pain, I know,
and the mountain is devoured up,
as mankind strikes each blow.

I watch from outcropped rock above.
Machines still rip and tear.
It's developers 'gainst nature,
and they don't seem to care.

So many days I've stood in awe
as nature played it's course,
and speechless from the things I saw.
Has 'Progress' no remorse?

I stand here with an aching heart.
All I can do is cry.
The mountain is no more for me;
I've come to say good-bye.

Almost Like Ol' Friends

A grand ol' buck all grizzled and gray,
for years I've been waiting for this day.
His antlers look like an ol' oak tree,
an' he just stands there in spite of me.
Years I've engaged in this pursuit,
yet somehow now, I just can't shoot.

I 'member 'im in his first year,
a spunky little fork-horned deer.
The years went by as I watched 'im grow.
A record book buck . . . I'm the hunter though.
To day is his day . . . I'm thinkin', ya know?
I think, "I'm gonna let 'im go."

Not to Worry

There's a question women utter
as they so often sputter
'bout the absence of their husband in the fall .

His household chores neglected.
His family feels rejected.
And he don't seem to hang around at all.

His inattentiveness
is causing you distress.
His priority should be you, after all.

He's up before the sun,
though not a thing gets done,
and you figger that he sure has got the gall.

Well, he sure seems unfettered
and you, you're gettin' weathered.
You feel like you could just sit down and bawl.

Your whole life could shatter.
It wouldn't seem to matter.
He acts as if he doesn't care at all.

You've resigned to let it go.
He doesn't care and doesn't know,
as he heads out to answer nature's call.

In retrospect you'll see.
You've fretted needlessly.
His love for you is always standin' tall.

He needs time in the wild.
His thoughts there are compiled.
It's time like these, he knows he has it all.

As he sits up in his stand
and looks about the land,
It's the memories of you that he'll recall.

So there's no need to fret
'bout the absence you regret,
and his time out in the woods, when it comes fall.

There's a smile upon his face,
as his mind begins to race,
and his memories of you begin to call.

As he hunts about the land,
just know that he's your man.
And when it comes to love, you have his all!

Where's My Husband?

And here I am with my bow fully drawn,
my sights on a buck at the break of dawn.
First day of the season, it could end right here,
but no, for now, I'll pass on this deer.

All year I dream of my time in the stand,
to checkout old haunts, maybe hunt some new land.
This buck's a nice un, but he'll have to wait.
And he'd better git goin' 'fore it's too late.

I could tag him right now, take 'im home, show the wife.
Then I'd have no reason to stay out of her life.
She says all season how she misses me so,
But complains when I'm home. . . . Ooh, I'll never know.

They say absence makes the heart grow fonder,
so I think I'll spend some time out yonder.

Potter County

In Northern Pennsylvania
as the summer turns to fall,
it's awful hard to concentrate
when the woods begin to call.

Now, I been the whole world over,
an' I seen a lot of things.
I bin to all those places
they say is fit fer kings.

But here in Potter County,
in these Allegany hills,
out there in the backwoods,
is where I get my thrills.

When the ridges set ablaze,
with nature's fiery show,
if there's a better place
I surely wouldn't know.

Gettin' High

A hunter sits up high in the trees
with adrenaline filling his arteries.

The beating of his heart,
the shaking of his knees,
all symptoms of this desired disease.

Nature's rush, as it's meant to be,
perched up high, in an ol' oak tree.

Camouflaged

A swallow perched upon my bow,
as I sat and watched a doe.
A funny bush, he didn't know.
He stopped to check me out, although,
he opted for another bough.

Sensing Nature

Have you ever felt a sunset,
as you sat and watched in awe
amazed at Mother Nature
and all the things you saw?

Victory

The doe stood there.
She flicked her tail.
She didn't have a chance.

I am the gracious predator,
mine is the victory dance.

That Old Familiar Feeling

There's an old familiar feeling
that comes at summer's end.
It comes along each year
just like a welcome friend.

Just as the leaves are changin',
and the kids are back in school,
I head on out to the forest.
It's like a golden rule.

My memories are of dreams fulfilled
and thoughts of hunts to come.
They occupy my cluttered mind
and not much work gets done.

I know the cure's out there . . . somewhere.
Time in the woods I s'pose.
Don't ask, how long it takes,
For sure, God only knows.

I'll do a little huntin', then
the feelings may subside,
but they'll all come back next year . . .
emotions I can't hide.

One More Time

When my time is over
and my huntin' days are done,
Lord, take me one more time
where nature and I were one.

Take me to the woods where
the game runs wild and free.
I'd like to sit just one more time
up in that ol' oak tree.

And hear the owls 'fore daybreak,
then crows throughout the day.
And I could even tolerate
an occasional blue jay.

If you don't mind, just one more time,
to the stand called number seven.
I guess you could say it's on the way,
Lord, it's just this side o' heaven.

43

The Ol' Flintlock
from a pioneer's perspective

He shuffles slowly through the powdery snow.
On his face, he feels the wind bite as it blows.
With cold steel and hardwood firm in his grip,
he crests the rise and scans the next dip.

The buck lay bedded his back to the wind.
His face obscured by a big oak limb.
He can tell by the points and the size of his rack
It must be "the buck" that makes that big track.

So far he's avoided the ol' buck's eye.
His flintlock is poised and his powder is dry.
Now him an' his rifle bin together fer life.
It's kept meat on the table for him an' his wife.

His flintlock's aimed, now the slow steady squeeze.
Click, fizz, BOOM! The buck struggles to his knees,
Then collapses, . . . and falls to the ground . . .
The woods deathly quiet, now void of all sound.

He's happy, yet saddened, by the big buck's defeat.
Yet the buck will provide his family with meat.
Predator and prey form a very close bond;
for this he is gracious and definitely fond.

The Provider

I sit here in this blustery storm,
here in this tree, just tryin' to stay warm.
Bin here since before the first light;
not sure why, but it sure feels right.

The weatherman promised this storm would soon pass,
and I want to be here, when the deer move, at last.
There's a foot of new fallen snow on the ground.
Their steps will be muffled. They won't make a sound.

I check my watch and wiggle my toes;
then I take off a glove so I can warm up my nose.
Got one candy bar left and my trail mix is gone.
Just three more hours, I gotta hang on.

I look to the west; I see clouds givin' way.
Just as promised . . . it's gonna be a good day.
Birds are out now . . . flyin' all around.
There's squirrels scurry'n' 'bout down on the ground.

BB

In the blackberry bushes, movement catches my eye.
I feel warm from adrenalin; it's the hunter's high.
It's that big buck, I've *bin* waitin' to see,
and he's comin' this way, headed straight for me.

My heart's beatin' louder as he gets within range.
Oh, I love this feelin' that some would think strange.
Startled by the impact and the unfamiliar sound,
he bolts thirty yards, then stops to look around.

He paints the snow red as blood pumps from his heart.
It's a predator's job and I've done my part.
Emotions, and feelings . . . uncontrollable urges;
I'm cold but I'm sweatin,' as adrenalin surges.

I feel kinda dizzy, and my hands begin to tremble.
Yet despite all of this, I still feel humble.
The Creator has bestowed upon me
the challenge, the thrill and the victory.

LORD, let us give thanks,
for meat on the table.
And too for the fact that
I'm here and I'm able.

BB

47

Savor the Moment

The afternoon sun
shines warm on me
as I'm perched in my
stand, here in this tree.

An eight point buck
is bedded just outa range.
Now I know that some
would think this strange.

But I don't care
if I get this buck,
'cause I've been blessed
with such good luck.

Hunts may come
and hunts may go . . .
to savor a moment
this long though . . .

You gotta hunt
for quite awhile,
so I'll just sit here
in the sun, and smile.

Disappointment

The biggest buck that I ever did see,
My arrow flew straight,
right into a tree.
Whoa is me, and the buck ran free.

How do I deal, how do I cope?
I'm twenty up and I feel like a dope.
My problems could be solved
with a short piece of rope, . . . Nope!

I think I'll just sit fer awhile
till sumpin' happens to make me smile.
I'll ponder life and all that's in it,
and still love the game, e'en though I can't win it.

*By the way it's not normally my luck
but last time this happened I got a bigger buck*
.

Confidence

I've been practicin' and practicin'
by shooting my new bow.
I'm buildin' up my confidence
to take whitetailed doe.

If Mother Nature smiles on me,
then it might just get done.
But if the chance ain't offered,
then it was just fer fun.

To hunt and be successful
takes more than shootin' straight.
Ya gotta find the right place
and ya better not be late.

You must blend in with nature
and not smell like a man.
You gotta know your prey
and how they use the land.

But confidence don't mean nuttin'
if nature were to intervene,
like when an arrow hits a twig
that you ain't never seen.

The wind may blow real steady;
it'll come right out of the west.
But fickle winds will take your plans
and lay 'em all to rest.

Another Year

It's over . . . gone at last.
With some regret, the season's passed.
Thoughts and memories fill my mind
of the good times left behind.

Most folks are lookin' forward
to the Christmas holidays.
But me . . . I'm lookin' backward
on a mornin's autumn haze.

To when the fog was liftin',
and a movement caught my eye.
It was that big ol' buck,
but he managed to slip by.

In solemn relaxation now,
I've got my freezer filled.
I think of huntin' buddies
and the game that I have killed.

As important as the ones I've shot,
are those that got away.
Then, there're the challenges
I faced on any given day.

Soon my thoughts and memories,
of hunts in seasons past,
will be replaced with plans and dreams
of future hunts at last.

Cabin Fever

Cabin fever's settin' in.
I don't know where to turn.
Can't sit still or concentrate,
just seem to itch and burn.

I think of hunts I had last fall
and a place to hunt this spring.
I just can't wait to get out in the woods
and hear those turkeys sing.

Winter Fits

Itching and burning
Tossing and turning,
I can't sleep a wink.
Can't even straight think.
Have trouble to talk
and sometimes can't walk.

My wife says cabin fever,
but ya know I don't believ 'er.
I wish there was a shot
'cause I get like this a lot.
The only known cure
is nature for sure.

La-Z-Boy™ Blues

Turkeys gobblin' all around,
the big tom's comin' in.
Adrenalin flows; if luck holds out,
I think this time I'll win.

The old tom is close by.
He is just outa sight.
We're talkin' a trophy
if I play my cards right.

As subtle as ol' tom takin' flight,
my dog jumps up in my lap.
It was then I awoke and realized,
I wasn't hunting . . . but takin' a nap.

**These winter blues have got a hold
and ya know they won't let go.
I sleep and dream of hunts to come
and awake to four feet of snow.**

Local Lore

In between all of the hunting seasons,
the stories and memories abound.
It helps keep our dreams in the heavens,
while our feet must remain on the ground.

Summer days long hot and muggy,
much too hot to scout.
Maybe I'll take my trusty ol' pickup,
and I'll have a look about.

I'll drive around the backroads,
check the fields and fence lines some more.
I finish the last of my supper,
kiss the wife, and head out the door.

As I drive down a dusty ol' road,
and I look to the top of a hill,
I remember a frosty fall mornin',
and a tag that never got filled.

The buck was a regular legend,
a topic of local lore.
The boys swappin' lies talked about 'im,
down at the local store.

As for me, it happened at midday;
I was bored and got caught off guard.
The buck came out of nowhere,
broadside and twenty five yard.

I just sat there and stared right at 'im,
and he in turn stared at me.
Then he melted off into the brush
behind some old oak tree.

I may drive around for hours,
maybe stop and see some friends.
But all the while I'm scoutin'
'cause the huntin never ends.

The Earth Don't Need Us

The earth is going to be here
long after we are gone.
It doesn't take a genius
to see that something's wrong.

We don't need to save the earth.
We need to save mankind,
to stabilize this mess,
before we're left behind.

We did not inherit earth
from our great forefathers.
We are only borrowing it
from our sons and daughters.

Taken from an old tribal proverb: "We did not inherit the earth from our parents; we are borrowing it from our children."

The Farmer's Market

Two hunters meet and then discuss,
the events that are so dear to us.
They talk of plans and old oak stands.
They reminisce of shots they missed.
First day is near, the weather's clear,
they're sure it will be brisk.

It's time to part, and with a start,
they begin to say good luck,
But then withdraw, and hem and haw,
for words they just seem stuck.
If their tags are filled on the first day,
Well then, . . . they're done huntin' fer buck.

Encounter with a Mountain Man

He had a wild and weathered look,
the kind you don't get from a book.
You see the teeth that nature took
as he steps grinning from the brook.

His smell, you probably wouldn't savor.
The wind . . . aren't cha glad, is in your favor.
He starts toward ya and ya never waver,
'cause you brought 'im soap 'n' a brand new shaver.

Another Day Gone

It's late afternoon
as the sun's settin' low.
Shadows hide in the darkness,
as the day gets ready to go.

You can feel the night creep slowly
as the daylight runs toward the west.
You hate to see it go, but ya know,
You've given it your best...

*. . . and the last remaining streaks of sun
crown the treetops, then it's done.*

The Wind is Your Friend

With wind in my face and
the sun at my back
I took off
on the ol' buck's track.

A couple of valleys
and one steep hill,
I topped the ridge;
there the buck lay still.

And just as I was takin' aim,
call it fate or call it strange,
that fickle wind,
it took to change.

I felt the wind
on the back o' my head.
Just then the buck bolted
from his new found bed.

I know it seems sad
that the buck got away,
but thanks to the wind
my workload was lighter that day.

The Pessimist and Optimist

The Pessimist and Optimist
appear to disagree.
Their perspectives seem quite contrary,
and that we all can see.

But take a closer look;
It may not be as it seems.
"I have found a point, and they concur,"
the moderator gleams.

The Optimist is certain,
he emphatically will state.
"This world in which we live,
there are none just quite as great."

The Pessimist, he nods his head,
as if he might agree.
"You have a valid point here,
I am afraid that it might be."

*Taken from the saying that, "The optimist believes we live in the best of all
possible worlds, and the pessimist fears that may be true."*

63

ELMBROOK CAMP, WINSLOW HILL, ELK COUNTY, PENNSYLVANIA

Tribute to Elmbrook

Way up in old Elk County,
on top of Winslow Hill,
when the bulls begin to bugle,
time seems to stand right still.

At a little camp called Elmbrook,
in the middle of this sanctuary,
you'll feel like you're in heaven,
be it June or January.

The eerie sounds of the buglin' bulls
that break the silent still,
shake the very core of my soul
and I pray they always will.

The Old Homestead

One day while I was huntin'
I stumbled upon this place.
It was where our predecessors dwelled
or so I assumed was the case.

The old home is long since gone,
a fireplace is all that remains,
and some remnants of a foundation
of the lives that progress claims.

This was home to a settler's family.
They raised their kids, and like us had their fights,
but around this fireplace they'd gather
together on blustery and cold winter nights.

Time goes and waits for no one.
This is proof that exceptions are nil.
They bore life's burdens and drove on,
for they had a settler's will.

Their trials and tribulations were many
and like us, they had aches and pain,
with no doctors or drugs to treat 'em.
It was all they could do to maintain.

They knew not of the civilized comforts
that we all take for granted today.
Aches and pains were taken in stride,
and they assumed that's the way it would stay.

They had work to do and they did it,
and you'd never hear 'em complain,
'cause all day long the work was tough
and every day was the same.

They'd celebrate when things went right,
and then when things went wrong,
they'd persevere, try a little harder,
and maybe sing a song.

It's nice to speculate and dream
of how things were back when,
but the truth remains, we'll never know.
So just be thankful, then!

The stories they'd tell,
if these rocks could talk,
about this place,
I've chosen to walk.

As we all know, what makes the memories are the special situations, sometimes adverse, sometimes humorous, and always at our friends' expense. It's the people that we chose to spend our time with. The bonds and friendships that develop are sometime peculiar at best. It often leads to a lot of good hearted jokes. Here's one of mine.

My Hero

My huntin' camp's where
I like to roam.
It is, in fact,
my Mother's home.

The comforts there are
the best by far.
I'm not sure why,
but they just are.

Now, speakin' of the comforts,
they start right at the door.
I've friends that drive a hundred miles
to sleep upon her floor.

And, just how is the huntin'?
Well, I'd say its mighty fine.
But 'tween the naps an' eatin'
we barely have the time.

One day right after lunchtime,
while nappin' o' so fair,
The sound of a roarin' chainsaw
shook me from my chair.

My ol' buddy Alvie
was sleepin' on the floor.
I thought, enough of this,
an' I headed out the door.

Once more I checked my back trail
but Alvie wasn't near.
So while he laid there nappin',
I went out and shot a deer.

Now, he don't think its funny
when I relate this story,
but if he'd stayed off the floor
he wouldn't have to worry.

This is a true story and that's pretty much the way that it happened.
My friend insisted that I put it in the book. I think that he just
wanted to get his name in here. Anyways, a special thanks to my
good buddy, Alvie, for all the memories, past and future.

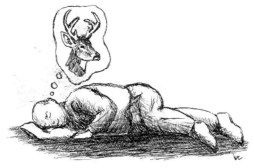

Science or Art

Some say huntin's a science,
While others say it's an art.
To study hard or be creative,
Why this just tears me apart.

I study hard by readin'
Huntin' stuff all the time.
And there's no doubt I'm a little creative,
By the way I twist a rhyme.

I once wrote a poem,
then I shot a real nice buck,
But when I think about it,
I'd have to chalk that up to luck.

One time I studied some deer sign
And I sat there for quite awhile,
But people kept driving by,
And all they did was smile.

Now as fer the methods of huntin'
Time tested and proven is luck.
And as for that art and science
Well I don't really care for it.

Another Banner Year

Here the fawns come trotting through
and now the does come in,
I'm waiting for that big ol' buck,
that's when the fun begins.

I saw him once last summer,
then early on this Fall.
His rack is big and wide and thick,
and most of all, it's tall.

Those tines go o'er half a foot,
their the lightest shade of bone.
With smaller bucks in his entourage,
He's rarely seen alone.

It's comin 'bout that time o' year,
It's gettin' near the rut.
I'll have to pass on smaller bucks,
hope I can make the cut.

But when I pass the test
and my patience has been shown,
I'll load that buck into my truck
and take my trophy home.

But if I hunt all season long
and never tag a deer,
The memories are what make this
another banner year.

RK Cafe'

Down past Billy Bob's Bar & Grill,
is a place called the Road Kill Café.
Whatever gets hit and lays on the road,
determines the special that day.

The food is in a class all of it's own,
and I quote the "Redneck gourmet,"
With entertainment divine, overhead anytime,
The buzzards perform a ballet.

Carcasses fresh
from the middle of the road
Bring em in by the truck,
and they'll take the whole load

The menu changes constantly,
and all throughout the day.
I never try to plan ahead;
I usually, just have the buffet.

The food is always plentiful.
You'll never find slim pickin',
and it all tastes so delicious.
Some say, "Just like chicken!"

And if you think the meat taste *fowl*,
and you're sittin there lookin dumbstruck.
Billy Bob might stop and explain,
"That's probably cause it's a duck."

There is rarely any seafood,.
maybe a turtle here and there.
It's mostly deer squirrel and rabbits,
and sometimes even a bear.

The kitchen crew at this kindly café
will cook anything for a buck.
When you ask them how the burgers are;
They'll say it's the finest ground "chuck."

The variety here is endless.
They serve frogs n toads 'n' snakes.
Have whatever you like, and follow it up
with their world famous chipmunk cupcake.

Those cooks work really really hard ,
and they work all kinds of hours,
Just to live up to their motto,
which is:
"*From Your Grille To Ours!*"

Every once in awhile, when hunting, you seem to have moments when you are more in touch with everything on a spiritual level, and you see everything clearly. That is what "Destination" is about. Call it an epiphany or a spiritual moment, if you will.

Destination

As I struggle down life's road,
I stop to look around.
I shed my heavy load,
and recognize it's where I am bound,
and feel content that I am found.
I've been here many times before
and never knew
I'd knocked on heaven's door.

When you have participated in an activity, such as hunting, and developed that special bond with others, the passing of a fellow hunter seems more intense in certain ways, because you have communed in nature. From then on, you are never really hunting without them. You know there will always be something that brings a smile to your face as you recall the good times, as you pass their favorite stand, or some place they missed an easy shot, or maybe the spot that they got the big one.

A Hunter's Farewell
A solemn face, his soul is bared,
he mourns the passing of a friend.
Memories of hunts they shared,
a bond that goes beyond the end.

*Dedicated to family and friends,
that hunt with us in spirit, now.*

This is a short story that I wrote,
when the ability for rhyme & meter escaped me:

The Buck of my Dreams

The fog is starting to come in. I've been in my treestand for about forty five minutes or more. Daylight is just beginning to overtake the darkness. I like to settle in about an hour before daybreak just to watch the woods come alive. The fog becomes thicker, and I can barely see twenty yards now. The moisture penetrates the warmth that I have accumulated climbing this tree, and I shudder. I notice how the smell of autumn in the woods somehow intensifies in the fog. I think about where a deer might come from and how they might appear. I always rehearse different scenarios to pass the time, but it never happens that way.

Wait! It almost looks like something in that opening to my right. . . . There's movement! Yes! I can make out the form of a deer. My heart skips a beat, and then I settle down. It's probably a doe, I think to myself. I am not here for just any deer. I am here for a large buck that haunts these woods. I caught a glimpse of him a couple of times this summer. In this fog, though, all I can see is an outline, even at twenty yards. Still, I am an optimist, and I have my bow ready to draw. Again, I tell myself, it's probably just a doe, and soon a couple of last spring's fawns will appear. The deer is at ten yards now. With the brush and fog obscuring my view, I can just see an outline of its back above the brush. But with the gaining light, I will know soon. As I look behind it for the fawns, it lifts its head. Oh boy! There is no more guessing now. This is the big one! Each long polished point on his heavy white rack is visible. I wait. One more step and he will expose his vitals. My bow is at full draw now.

In the distance, someone is hollering. The buck alerts then melts into the brush, which in turns melts away also. Then I hear the hollering again. It's my wife's voice, "Honey, where are you?" Slowly, I return to reality, and my living room, with half a cup of cold coffee in my trembling hand. I've been blindly staring out the window at three feet of fresh snow on this February morn.

While I recompose myself, the wife says, "I could have sworn you were in another world." "Yeah . . . yeah, I guess I was," as I manage to speak. Then she reminds me, "You'd better get going. You'll be late for work."

Step into the Cabin,
and come on in the Kitchen.

The cycle of life
is not complete,
until we have
sat down to eat.

I know we all like to eat, and any hunting story wouldn't be complete until a favorite recipe is exchanged. Here is one of mine:

CROCKPOT VENISON & MUSHROOMS

3 lbs. of venison cut into bite size pieces, about 1 inch cubes, or drained canned venison.
3/4 cup of red cooking wine
1 pkg of onion soup mix
1 can of golden mushroom soup
1 can of cream of mushroom soup
1 to 3 cups of fresh or canned sliced mushrooms

Put everything together in the crock pot, mix it up, and cook for about 10 to 12 hours on a low setting, then on high for the last hour or so. Serve it over noodles, rice, or potatoes. I use egg noodles. For some added zing, you can top with sour cream or plain yogurt before serving.

Enjoy